LIFE LESSONS FROM YOUR KNICKER DRAWER

Declutter your head, transform your life

KERRY HALES

authors
AND CO.

Dedication

For you

A large dose of intention and a dollop of fun, you can create a life you love!

Contents

Acknowledgements

There are so many to thank.

Mum
I know you won't read this, but as you were my biggest supporter. So many times, you told me, 'You are so smart you can do anything'. This book is the testament that, you know, you were right mum! Blimey, I wish you were here to give you a copy. I'd sign it too!

Frank
For your belief in me and my coaching and for seeing a vision of what this funny insightful book will do and why it needed to come to life. Thank you.

Proofreaders
There are so many of you. Thank you for sharing your brilliance with me. Mostly Oak for sharing your wisdom and pouring it onto the cover.

Friends

I have bored you silly for years. I think you will be saying, 'TFFT, maybe she will stop talking about it now!' Thank you for your patience. Until the next time…

My fabulous clients

The funny thing about this book is when you work with me, you all know how much I use analogies in my work and how powerful they are in creating change. It was when I found a universal one in 'knickers', I knew that this book could work.

Business buddies

Wow, there is a long list and I know I will forget someone who is searching for their name. I am inspired and scared by you all most days. Some more than others.

Authors & Co and Destination Inspiration Mastermind

This book would still be sitting ruminating around my head for another six years or more if I had not said yes to joining you. I cannot even begin to say thank you enough for making me birth this book. I want and need to thank you for it. Life will never be the same again.

Everyone else

I send you love and gratitude for being part of the journey. Let the fun continue.

Introduction

Please God, no. I stared for some time. In front of my full-length mirror, in my bra and knickers, for what felt like a life-time, I stood and stared. The woman looking back at me was not 'me' and I was clearly not her. I was not connected to this woman. She was not who I was. But I was curious to know… Who the hell was she then? Because, sure as shit, she was not the girl I was inside.

I stood there as an overweight 45-year-old woman, wearing my dead mothers' knickers and a bra that had two of the three catches broken. I kid you not. My mother died from cancer that had ravaged her body for three years. Her symptoms made her itch terribly and because of this, she tried different knickers all the time, *hoping* they would feel comfortable – they didn't. Truth is, in the end she went commando – if that isn't ironic, I don't know what is; when you feel the least sexy in your life, you go without knickers…

There I stood in a pair of white 'high cut briefs' that used to belong to my 70-year-old mother, and I wondered why I didn't recognise myself. I can see now it was hardly surprising.

How did I get there? How on earth did 'I' get there? The girl who had just told her coach, when asked how she wanted to feel about her body, "sexy, lean and strong" was not the version I saw in the mirror. This was the opposite of who I was underneath. It hurt. I felt I had let myself down. I had let go of who I was in my life, and this was a visual reflection of that. The manifestation of my life was before me. I just stared at her. Who was 'this' woman? There was disgust. There was sadness. I cried and stood there sobbing for a while to let it all out: the desperation, the 'woe is me', the anger, the story of how what I wanted was not what I had… and the reality that this girl was not 'me'.

Yes, I was grieving – my mum had died just four months earlier - but I was also a sadder and fatter version of the sexy, strong, smart and sassy spirit I knew I was. But she was on the inside, and that didn't reflect what I saw on the outside. She was well hidden. She was hiding and hurting.

But part of me knew that this was significant, and for some bizarre reason I took a photo of 'her'. I know now that this was the turning point for me, but at that time, I just looked and wondered who *she* was. This old woman with her mum's knickers on, wanting to be something that she was not.

Do you want to be someone different than who you are but don't know where to start? Or perhaps, like me, you have so much in life and who are you to say this is not enough, I am not happy? I know it was my moment and this may be yours too. For when I looked at what I wanted and it wasn't what I had, I knew there were changes that had to be made.

So, this was my moment. And I knew it was going to take some change. Because this was not who I was and as that was what I did for a living, I knew I had some work to do. By realising this was not me, that this was not how I wanted to feel, I knew changes had to be made.

My new declaration was "I have a 'Sexy, Lean and Strong body!" It was going to be the new me and I was excited.

The accumulation of knickers in your drawers is such a reflective space of life. How many pairs do you have in life that you no longer use? If you have full drawers of old knickers you are likely to be craving space to think in life. No space to think or to create a life you truly want? It will be reflected in many areas of your life – including the knicker drawer. It is a space that is very personal to women, it just doesn't have the same impact in men. It is women's emotional core. It is an intimate look into the world of a how a woman feels about who she is.

As you go through this book, it is my intention for you to look at this one part of your life as a reflection of the others. It will shine a light into the parts of your life that you still have stories attached to, that you have lots of feelings about - a memory that you cherish, a desire to feel more of something that is missing. Or it could the opposite. It could be full of avoidance - lots of shameful things that you want to cover up and deny. The recognition to just notice what letting go of these items does to your thinking can be enough to release it. Maybe you think about saying goodbye with love to release that energy – clear that space in your head so you can then create what you want now. It may bring up uncomfortable memories (old thinking) and it may evoke emotions. But for this, I am going to share with you some journaling tips to get you through it.

There is such a strong connection to this drawer, more than any other in a woman's life, but the impact of investigating it will allow you the space to create clarity in all areas of your life. When you understand your particular story, it will appear everywhere in your life – the one that keeps you safe – the one that you can blame for why your life is not happening how you want it to. The story that says, it's ok, we know it wasn't your fault and this happens because of that. But I am here to say, what if it were possible to get curious about life and just let go. If you have the courage to do this, there is so much more on the other side for you.

Once you have this nugget of truth – the story that you thought was your life, that you thought you had no responsibility for – and you take back your power, you reclaim that space where you get to say…

"THIS IS WHAT I WANT, for me'. For ME. For this is *my* time here. And yes, shitty things have happened. And yes, I did allow myself to feel that for a long time - years have gone by. But now I see it. This is MY time, and I shall take back my life!

And as mad as it seems you CAN do this through your knicker drawer, just by noticing and acting on that. A simple, yet profound way to take responsibility for creating a life you want, in easy steps.

The reason I want to share my story is that I was literally standing there in a pair of a 70-year old's knickers. And it was NO joke. I was NOT laughing. I can laugh now, but then? #funnynotfunny.

So I am sharing this story for you to laugh and learn more about who you are through your knickers. We have so much attachment to these small garments, we attach so many meanings to them. Having told my story to many of my friends, I realised that it has enabled many of them to look at their knicker drawer and to see their life before them.

I love using analogies when I am coaching and this simple story of my knicker drawer, and what unfolded following my realisation, allowed me and many others to look at their lives through their knicker drawer. I know, it sounds so crazy, but believe me when you next look in that drawer and then ask your friends, let them tell their stories of the stuff they keep, and then ask how that is connected to their lives…

Over a glass of wine, it will no doubt be one of those conversations that are deep yet hilarious… and who doesn't want one of those with your besties?

I have a real distaste of waste. Probably why I chose to be a project and change manager in the NHS, to eliminate wasted time. I see my role as a coach in very much the same way. How does each and every communication create change in a way that gets to the point required, as effectively and efficiently as possible. So, as much as this may 'feel' like a funny little book, do not underestimate what it will do for you. I pour all my wisdom into each of my projects. A reformed perfectionist.

My PROMISE to you is that if you give me your attention for a few hours, I will give you back years of your life. Years you may otherwise continue to waste on thinking about stuff that has no bearing on your present life or happiness. In fact, if you read this book and do the simple tasks at the end of each section – it will take you no longer than a few hours - you will feel and start to live differently. AND this book is for you to share with your girlfriends. Not this actual book. Buy them one and then ask them what they noticed. In that simple conversation, you will get an insight into your girlfriends like never before.

In each section I will take you on a journey of discovery and each stage gives you an opportunity to get curious about where else you notice these patterns.

In section one, we notice that you never really clear things out. We often skim over what we want but to go deep down into what is really there... we get uncomfortable and let ourselves off. We back off. But this time, we are backing IN. This time I am going to be with you, and I want you to understand that there are only habits. The 'good' or 'bad' parts are what you will notice. For example, if you are overly fussy about something that really doesn't matter, that's a waste of your attention and it's not going to give you the results you desire. But if you put that attention into something that is a bigger challenge, it will show you the results you want.

In section two, we are going to fill in your life with what you want. A different kind of filling your life up. A consciousness that you haven't felt before. No more stuff to blind you so you can't see what you don't like, no more 'busyness' going on, so you don't have time to do something about it. This section will fill your cup up with loving who you are and what you want.

In the last section, we are going to talk about what you love and find fun. Yes, we may get a little sexy in there but in truth I want you to love that fun side of you again and look at taking responsibility for what you have. Once you see this, you will set your standards higher, and be more connected to your responsibility for creating what you want.

Finally, we put all you have learnt together in a plan. A plan that allows you to see what you want, from now on, with your newfound curiosity of who you are today - without any old knickers and odds and sods clogging up your life!

I am so excited for you to step into discovering more about who you are and the adventures that this will bring. It is only a short read away. Grab a pen, some paper and let's go!

Some words from a client of Kerry's

 "Just so that you're not under any illusions from the start... Kerry is a life changer. She is brilliant!

I had lost my identity years ago, but finally got it back and it's because of Kerry (and me of course, but she definitely had something to do with it!) Kerry is there, discussing, motivating, changing, listening. There is just something about the way she is, the way she works with you. Kerry helped me to find me again and I love being me!

So here I was six months ago... self conscious, non confrontational, too scared to be me, scared of people judging me, not allowing myself to express myself, too controlling, holding back the things I'm good at, not even knowing what I was good at or if these things really and truly existed, never letting myself relax and have fun, not letting go and being creative with my strengths, letting my weaknesses eat me up, not letting my daughter be herself, bowing down to those I thought were higher up than me, not respecting myself... The list goes on, it's so negative.

Yes, some of these negative things are actually part of me and that's ok, but it's learning how to feel good about the things I want to be and working on letting go of the things I don't want to be.

She has a way of helping you figure it out for yourself. 'She's got the knack (and a whole host of animated expressions to go with it!)

So, after six months, I actually love myself and don't feel selfish for it. My family have seen the difference. 'It's a work in progress, but I'm excited to go forward now rather than analyse too much of the past. Everyone has it in them to be great, Kerry just helps you find it.

Thank you from the bottom of my heart."

Jules

Section One - What do you have in there?

Follow me into the world of your underwear drawer and you will find wisdom and humour in your life too!

This book may have a funny title and I am all for having fun while we do anything in life, but this is a book to transform your life with. Yes, we are going to use the analogy of your knicker drawer, but there is a solid reason behind this. In my coaching practice, I use analogies connected to your life and this helps you to see life differently. But there is a universal analogy we can use for women that holds so much of our emotional attachments found in our underwear. We will touch upon those and how you feel about your body, as well as learning about the patterns we have in such a personal space that can be a revealing connection to who we are in other areas of our lives. Be prepared to laugh and cry. This is a journey of discovery into who you are today and to love, really learn to love, you, just for being **you**. And the by-product of this is that you are going to feel fabulous in your underwear forever more – after a little shopping trip!

Before we start the transformation, I want you to do what I did, because sometimes we just get used to seeing what we see now as normal and I want to make sure you 'see' your transformation, as well as feel it. It may feel weird, but I need to ask you to do this. As soon as you can, go and take off your clothes apart from your knickers and bra and stand in front of a full-length mirror. Breathe. It is just you and me, and I know how uncomfortable that may feel. There may be a lot of thinking involved in this, and you will already have visions of what you 'think' you will look like. But we need to start somewhere.

Take a good look and write down what you are wearing now. Share as much detail as you can, what emotions come up when you look at you. What underwear are you wearing? How old is it? What do you feel about it? I want you to really own who she is, from a curious as possible space. Like it was your best friend describing you. So you can just be as factual as possible describe them, even if it's one pair of grey knickers, about two years old, loose around the edge:

_____

_____

_____

_____

_____

_____

_____

Well done you.

If you decided to skip this, please go back and write out why. Is this something you do often? Have a good idea but decide to only do it half mast, so the outcomes aren't traceable back to you? "Well, I kinda did it…" or maybe it is "oh, I will do that later, when no one is here".

Or perhaps you just skim over it thinking there will be easier parts to this book? Surely, she doesn't want me to take off my clothes!

Yes, I do. Why? Because change is uncomfortable. Why? Because we get familiar with our discomfort, and we like the comfort in that. I know it sounds weird but read it again. We like familiarity. And I want to interrupt that pattern. And once you do this, you can't go back.

Once you have stood there - just you – it will be like switching on a light. It will feel scary. But you will get through it. It will bring up emotions but remember that you CAN do difficult things. We all can. But sometimes we just get into a way of looking for ease when a little bit of pain is our best way forward.

So, please, I really beg of you to take a breath, say "shit" as many times as you need, and go do the exercise!

Right. You may now move on, feeling a little lighter and you are good to go!

Question: How do you *want* to feel about your body?

Just like I did, I would love for you to set an intention of how you would *like* to feel.

Write down your 'statement of intent'. Remember, yes this is connected to your body, but broaden this out to who you are.

My example had **stron**g in it. Because I knew I needed to be strong and resilient. My job is to be there for people and to hold a space. I need to be strong and to be able to hold a space for others to be whomever they need to be. I love what I do and who I surround myself with, but it does take conscious work to make sure I keep open and creating. It takes me being strong in my body and mind.

What is that for you? Who do you need to be to be able to fulfil your role and dreams?

I, _____ have a _____,

_____ and _____ body!

(you)(Adjective)(Adjective)(Adjective)

I will ask you again in each section, but this is our intention for you. Keep coming back to this. Write it out on a post it and stick it places – in your purse and in your journal. This is what is real for you. Do not listen to the mind, which will undoubtedly start rambling after you have put pen to paper. It is your mind that will want to keep you safe. Uncomfortable, but safe. The fear will rise. With it will come all of the stories of why you need to stay as you are. Your ego loves certainty and uncertainty will poke it. It will not like it. My advice is to thank it politely and say – "Thank you for notic-ing, but I am going do this anyway."

Now, earlier I asked you to look in the mirror. You do not HAVE to look in the mirror, but it will really help if you do - not to notice everything that's wrong - do not judge. Not at all. I want you to look at and love whoever is there - she has been through so much and you should acknowledge that. It is about loving you in *all* of your wonderment. Take another look at your intention and confirm it to yourself. I will be alongside you throughout this book, but in truth, you could just read this and not do any of the exercises and see what happens… or you could really just pour yourself in to it, with a 'what do I have to lose' attitude. Give me your trust just for a few hours and then you can go back… if you can. In this moment I am asking you to let go of the control for this and trust this process.

Let's get to it.

In this section I am going to inject as much curiosity about your life and how it could be different as possible. When we think about changing our life, we can often think about the *whole* project – which will totally overwhelm you into procras-tination and often throw you back further with yet another failure of your desired change. This section is the start of the process, just a small step you can do to trick your mind (that never wants change and loves stability) into doing *one* thing. I promise that in each section there will be some mulling over to do and then some action taking. I will share some journal prompts for you to work through what you are noticing, any hesitation(s) you have, and how you can reframe these into a statement of intention of how you want to feel. Fun, easy, but most importantly, life changing.

The first step of change is being aware of what we actually have. Facing the 'truth of the matter' is not as simple as we like to think it is. There is a process to go through and I want to share this with you, so no matter where you are in the process, it will help to clarify where *you* are in the four steps of change, so you feel you are getting somewhere.

This critical part is sometimes all you need. A compass is great, but it is no good if you don't know where you are starting from.

In this book, we are using your knicker drawer, but the process is the same, no matter what you want to change. We are going to go slowly through this together – taking you from one stage to the next and learning as you go. Although these are known as 'stages' they may feel bigger when we write about them. But please know this, it can be as easy as turning on a light so you can now see something you didn't in the past.

Once you see it, you can't unsee it. It's a fast and simple way of change. And when we transfer those learnings into other areas of your life, it will be easier to see it. Because now you are aware of what you are looking for, or the 'outcome', it is easier to find. A goal rather than a feeling.

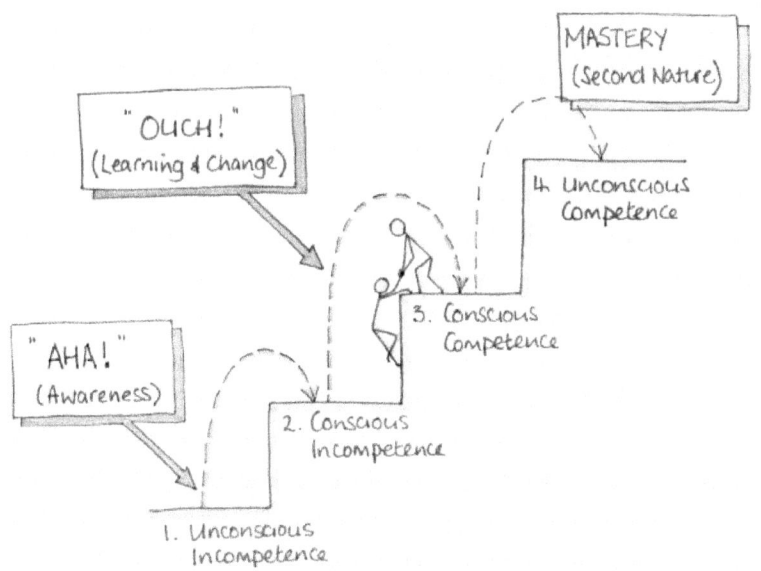

Stage One - Unconscious Incompetence:

Not aware there is a problem and that it has a significant impact on your life.

Stage Two - Conscious Incompetence:

Aware of the said problem, but still not sure what you can do about it.

Stage Three - Conscious Competence:

Aware of the problem and now you know what to do about it.

Stage Four - Unconscious Competence:

You now live in this new awareness without 'thinking' about it and you are doing it.

The good news about this chain of change is that you are already at Stage Two! Oh, I do like efficiency! Hence this is NOT a long book. I want you to get what you need and to go create it. You are here and you are curious to learn, right? Before opening this book you may have been unaware of how life could be different. Your desire for change may have even felt overwhelming. One thing for sure is that any change can be like that, but I want you to know that this is easy to implement, with such powerful results. Just stay with it.

I take change *very seriously* ok, but how we go about it does not mean we can't laugh as we learn. In fact, there are studies showing that having fun while you learn will increase your capacity to learn. I come from place of curious learning and experience of watching clients over the last 20 years. In a past life, I was also a project manager and I found the best way to implement a change is to think of it like a 'pilot' - a different way to see how it impacts your life and if you like it, do it more and if you do not like it, you can go back to how you were with a newfound love of your original way of living. A try it before you buy philosophy, if you like.

Your knicker drawer is going to add that fun part, but do not underestimate the feelings you have. It is going to get emotional in here. Please be prepared for that. I will be here to go with you – your emotions may come in waves, but I would be amiss not to mention this now. I shall explain more in your journal lesson of the day at the end of each section for you. But for now, just know that you are going into something that is fun. You are going to give it your all and then see what happens…

So we know we are in stage two – we are **aware** we have an 'issue' cluttering up our life. And now we want to get stuck in.

Firstly, I want you to make sure you have time to do this and be prepared. 'Project knickers' will really depend on how big your drawers are and much you have stored in there. Each item has a story attached to it and the stories of our lives can be indulgent. We get a lot of attention from the drama attached to the emotions of a story we have. The process will take you on a journey of discovery and in doing so, it will ask you to reflect on where else in your life you are doing the same 'function' but in a different form. Yes, we are talking about knickers. But I want to get you curious about what you might find.

I want you to notice what comes up for you. To look and see what you have created. Be proud. Own it. Feel it. Not as the Negative Nelly, who has her judgey pants on. We need to feel the feels and the emotions we have attached, and then we can move on. Part of letting go is seeing how strongly we hold onto uncomfortable things because they are comfortable in their familiarity. You know it is bad, you know it is not allowing you to love who you are, but you still do it. Right?

Here is an analogy I have often used to help with discovering what you are currently not seeing, and therefore not noticing its impact on you and your ability to create the space that allows change to happen.

I want you to think of your life as a playroom. Your 'Playroom of Life'. In that space, it is all your energy. It has all the things you want. All the things that make you feeeeel good. It has things in there that you can create, people you love, it inspires you to go be the person you can be. You absolutely love it in there. It is your space. It is home. It smells like you…

But hold on a minute…

"What is that in the corner?"

"Oh thaaaat,' you say sheepishly "that's just a pile of stuff that I don't use…"

"Oh! What is in it?" I ask curiously, but with intention.

"Well, I don't know really, and I don't want to talk about it, it has stuff that just is as it is…"

I am now eyeballing…and rolling them…

"Er. Ok. This is how this works. If we want your life to be running how you want it to be, we will need to look at what is **really** there. If there is 'stuff' in there, we need to get it all out and review it. There can be all kinds of 'woes', 'worries', 'shoulds' and stories and we need to look at them **all**. Turds in glitter are still turds. No matter how much you polish a turd, it is still a turd. And this journey is about noticing what you have agreed in your head that has no impact. So, noticing every little, seemingly insignificant thing. We need to clear them ALL out.

So, I shall ask you again, (with a smile) What do you have in there?", looking at a corner that has a pretty throw over it.

"But I have spent years making that corner of my life (room) ok with me."

"But this is a metaphor for your life and energy. If you are agreeing that you can't use part of you, that is spent on covering up old shit, you can't use that space for anything else… it is wasted space, stagnant energy. If you only have access to 75% of your room because of the old shit in the corner that has all the reasons to stay there, you are really saying that, in this life I now only have 75% to play with… for the rest of my life"

"Oh. Shit."

"Yeah. Shit. Now you know what it is costing you, we can do something about it. If you are ready to look under the throw? "

"I am slightly frightened and a bit irritated. What will we do with what I will find?"

"Yes, I know. It is scary. But the funny thing is that you are no longer the person you were when you put all the things you don't want deal with under the 'throw of shame'. You are no longer that person. And now the power that story and its emotions once had is not there anymore - unless you keep telling yourself it is and you reaffirm it. No matter what happened or when it happened, it is not here now, unless you make it so."

"Ah. I don't like it. I have a lot of reasons why it's in there."

"Yes, I know, but sometimes all we need to do to lift that old energy is to notice it, to work through some of the forgiveness, to thank it for what it gave you and be ready to work on letting it go, instead of holding onto it. Are you ready?"

"I think so…"

Before you go grab that drawer and we start the physical part; I have something for you to play with to get you curious about the stories you may find. Like I have said, it may be that when you see them, you are ready to let go, or there may be some that will take more work. Either way, know that you can do this and no matter what, you can, and will, feel the change very quickly. The easy wins will be there straight away. The harder ones may take more work and journaling and poking about to let them go, but if you have the courage, you can do this…

Journal Exercise:

In the list below, I want you to be as honest as you can be – this is your journey and as it is a book, no one will know if you play it from the surface or if you dig deep. I will ask you to dig as deep as you feel comfortable and if you want to revisit later, you can. But do give it a good dig around; I promise you the more you dig, the more you create. You're shovelling the shit out. Yeah, I said shit again. And this is where I want you to make your notes. It helps with making this yours. If you feel better about it, I would also consider burning this book after reading if you have really divulged some of your past that you want to let go. It is not a diary or journal that you need to keep.

A huge part of this is that, by letting go you truly do LET THAT GO. That includes this book. Write in it, scribble in it, draw over it – really embrace it as part of the process you are going through. Not a perfect book that doesn't look like it has been read. No, please… no. Let it be it dog eared and scruffy and then… you let it go. Yeah…

OK. Grab a pen. I want you to read each description of the knickers and note if you have *any kinds* of those described. Make notes. Ready?

Go.

Old times sake?

The memory of a time when life was "ahhhh" and it isn't like it is now…

Agreement: - Judging life for being better in the past.

For wishful thinking?

Kept in hope we will get to wear it again, the idea of what life 'would be' or 'could be' or 'should be'.

Agreement: - Used as a weapon of not being good enough.

Special occasions...

The suck you in and push you up, that you can only stand for a 'special' occasion when we want to look our **best** and need that extra little bit of help. Or again, if we are talking about holding on to some items that you never wear?

Agreement: - How many do you have of these and how often do you really use them? How many of one thing does one need? Bulking up space reduces our capacity to allow and to create what we want in the present.

Not supposed to be in there...

The misplaced emotionally attached items but they have been there so long that this is where they belong...

Agreement: - It's a sacred place that has so much more meaning to it than we are conscious of. Where is your safe space that precious items are kept hidden instead of shown?

_____

_____

_____

_____

_____

_____

No longer fit into...

These are what you loved and long to still wear.

Agreement: - remind you of the time when your body was a different, 'better' shape and yet you didn't appreciate it at the time...Another in the 'you don't have what you want category'.

_____

_____

_____

_____

_____

_____

Aspire to fit into...

Another blow to the you today. Shame and all that... but when you get it right and you do actually stop eating... at all! You may fit into them and therefore we keep them...

Agreement: That the future is there but will you ever get there? A constant reminder that you are 'not good enough yet...' a lure of what could be or might be, but not just yet...

Broken...

But if you could fix it... it would be amazing again... and so would you... The "if only" is there... that you just don't make time or want to make time to do this.

Agreement: Shame on you for not repairing something that meant so much at one time...What a reminder that you just don't find time for the things that are 'important', or were so.

Someone you love gave them to you

Oldest friend in the world bought it for you... can't do it. Won't do it. Shall not do it...

Agreement: That your happiness is second to a 'thought' that someone would want you to stay in a place because of them.

Agreement: That your life is less important than what you 'think' others may or may not think of what they gave you, when they gave it to you and for whatever reason they did – means you HAVE to keep it forever or they will never talk to you again. Ever. It's a crock! All lies.

Appreciating life when it is here is vital, and letting go of what 'was' will allow you to love what you have now. Because life is here. Now. And if you asked anyone who really loves you if they would mind you making space for you and your life, they may be a little 'oh', but never to the detriment to your happiness...

Most uncomfortable thing EVER…

But you bought it when you got a pay rise and therefore it is there to remind you that you are worthy!

Agreement: Representing a better you! Here it is. The forgiveness is essential when we are looking at our past as being the better time. Because that meanness inside that beats you because you are no longer her will continue – she is your inner bully. Facing her is going to take courage but we need to go there. You are a beautiful human, on this planet, now.

Inner bully is a bitch. She is never gonna be nice. EVER. So don't' expect her to say it will be ok. You have to be that person who says NO. I put me first.

Periods

Those pairs that are for when you have your period. They are usually old and err… grey! But we keep em. We wear em and they are never seen. Ever. By anyone other than our mothers and besties!

Agreement: This one gets me. I try. But I need to work hard on this one as it has so many connotations of what we feel about ourselves when we have our period. When I was younger, my mother told me under no circumstances do I leave blood in the toilet. She had been taught by her boarding school that this was 'women's business'. We have so much conditioned shame passed down to us and by us and the men who walk alongside us.

Love that you are part of the human race that gives birth and, as part of that magic, we celebrate our menstruation. Work through all the stories you have attached to this and get yourself some beautiful knickers that expand with your swollen tummy to be kind. It is essential to be kind to yourself during a time when your emotions can take a strong hold.

Ugliest thing in the world:

I hide it when I wear it, but I love it… why? Because you hardly notice you are wearing it when you do…. Surely all underwear should feel this good… but it didn't get to the looks department… and now it is grey, holey and shabby…

Agreement: That you are not worthy of finding something that you love and makes you feel wonderful.

Research your knickers – there are many varieties out there and there is one that fits this bill.

No One Sees...

These are the ones that only you get to see... but you would like to share. They need too much courage for you to wear them... and share them... lordy, no!

Agreement: That the real you is for your eyes only...

This is the courage to be you, wearing what you love, how you wear it. It is nobody else's business to tell you what you 'should' wear. Wear and be proudly you in whatever you love.

_____
_____
_____
_____
_____
_____
_____

Yours...

This is your space. Just for you. Add in here what you know you do and have...

_____
_____
_____
_____
_____
_____
_____

This is the courage to be you, wearing what you love, how you wear it. It is nobody else's business to tell you what you 'should' wear.

Appreciate the lesson

Spend time seeing what you have now. What is there, the life you had to get it to where it is. This is an important part of any change process and to get into the 'now' of life. It seems a simple enough exercise. But the whole part of what it teaches is vital in learning to love our life and who we are. Yes, this book is about knickers… but there is a message I would love for you to take away with you - to love what you have is vital because in this life there are so many variables out there. The one thing we can work on and be consistent in is you. The person who is sitting here reading a book about knickers. In this mad, mad, world we have, the one true thing we have is now. This moment. And there is only one you.

In the next section we are going get to the physical part of decluttering and the last part will be conscious filling up that cup with LOVE - setting up the foundations of your life for what you LOVE now.

Below are the journal prompts I want you to fill in with all of what you noticed. Really pour every little, seemingly insignificant, thing in here. It will lock in the learnings and awakenings you have had from what we have covered so far. The letting go can only happen if you notice what you are holding onto. So, use the checklist and really connect with what each list means for you. This list is not by far comprehensive. Every time I have discussed this with both clients and friends, they always add some of their own. Add yours too.

Journal Exercise:

To affirm your learning as we go through this journey, I would love for you to complete these four questions, or as I like to call them, prompts. Grab a pen and complete each one. Please, really share what came up for you because as we move through this journey, we will build on each section. The more you share, the deeper the learning. I find rules help, so if you ask yourself 'what else' at least three times, you will get into a space of just letting it out for the pure joy of it. Yes, I know it may feel clunky if you haven't done it before, but go with me and just let that pen do its job. Better out than in!

Let's go!

What kind of knickers do you know feel fabulous for you?

What kinds of those NOT described above do you have, that you now know you need to 'let go' of?

What is stopping you from having what you REALLY want to wear? (costs, agreements of how they look, what people have said, what you feel it will make you…)

Journal below any 'other' thoughts that come up from what we have talked about. This is out of left field, and you may just think 'oh, random', but NOTHING is. Get it down here. It is all great stuff. You may, by releasing stuff, allow a space for something magical to pop into your head. It could be a new idea, a solution to something you had been 'trying' to work on but just couldn't see it… anything is possible here in this space. Allow it all in. Say yes to it all.

Section Review.

Thank you for following this far. This was our first introduction into the many stories - your stories - that are reflected in our knicker drawer. Who knew, eh? But the truth is that how we do one thing is how we do many things – and that is the power that will come from going through this journey with me. The process of becoming DeKluttered™ is laid out in this and the coming sections.

To review:

We can simplify the list into four categories:

Used to's: All those who you beat yourself with that are from a past version of who you were.

Loved: I loved it when I bought it and it has amazing memories in it. But it does not serve me now.

Want to: I will wear it when… the universe turns flat… it is never gonna happen…

Wear now: Yes, I love it all. It feels like me and I feel awesome in it – our goal!

Notice what stories you have. This is the first step, to have the courage to say:

"No. Not anymore. I will not tolerate an outdated version of myself. I will now and forever more treat myself like my best friend. Because I love me."

It is time for your today to have its turn.

Some words from a client of Kerry's

 Kerry, Kerry, Kerry - say her name three times and amazing things will happen!

Once upon a time, she helped me to fish a turd out of the otherwise beautiful organic soup of my business and she has been helping others to shift the sh*t ever since! There is simply no better person to turn to when you're struggling to see a way through, if there are too many options in front of you, or if you just need someone to keep pushing you along and holding you accountable through this journey called "entrepreneurship".

We all need someone to have our backs, keep nudging us forward. It's not always comfortable or easy, but when you reach that Eureka moment, you'll wonder what all the fuss was about and then the true value in Kerry's coaching and support will properly be understood.

She can see the potential and ability in everyone she coaches, especially in the times when we are doubting ourselves and our own ability. Those are exactly the times when you need someone like Kerry in your corner.

I highly recommend Kerry, without hesitation.

Kate

2

Section Two - Declutter your drawer

In this section, we are going to set the foundation. Think of a house. If we kept a few dodgy foundations and built good around it, there would be subsidence at some point. Yes, we can keep some of the good stuff and recycle, but mostly it is going to be new, fresh and workable to who you are today.

The last section was about noticing – increasing your curiosity about what you have that isn't working in your life and how it impacts you. Once you notice this, we can now start the physical part of creating a life you want.

We are going to get physical and get into action. Which is what we need. Change can happen in your head, and that was the last section. Start to recognise the compromise that you have agreed in the past. It is ok not to have what you want, when you avoid finding what that is for you – because it is going to hurt. Or the idea it will be painful.

Follow this book through and I will be here with you. Opening up your life for you to feel more connected to who you are, to simplify your life and to enjoy it every day.

We are going to get physical today. You are going to need to put some time aside for this; 30 minutes should be ample. Be prepared to clean, have bags to let go, bags to recycle and an open mind.

Let's go!

Step One – Clear it ALL out.

Oh, here is some 'pre-work' I would like you to do – Line it! Create a liner. I know this may feel excessive, but we are reaffirming that there will be no compromising and when you take your underwear out of a drawer that looks and smells great – the day is starting right – not 'ok' or 'that'll do'. Just "ok" is not what you are here for. YOU are here to love you and all you do.

We can make a liner easily – or buy some ready-made that make you smile. Not 'that will do'.

Here's a simple guide to make your own:

Choose the paper you'd like to use – you may have some left-over wallpaper or card:

- Measure the inside of the drawer bottom you would like lined.
- Cut your paper to the desired size.
- Mix a water and essential oil mixture.
- Pour mixture into a clean spray bottle – or just dab!

- Mist the mixture onto your paper until completely damp
- Hang it on the line to dry – we don't want damp smelling anything… Do this first.

Now you are ready to clear it all out. I mean literally. Clear it out and breathe in the space of what it feels like to not have anything in there AT ALL. To literally start again. The purpose of this is to feel how you are choosing this. From this moment on, you know you are choosing what goes in. No matter what compromising you are doing, the choice is still there. It has to be an empty space.

Clean it. Really make it the best it can be. All the marks, dust, smell.

Make the drawer good. I.e. does it work well, does it need some wax on the bottom on the drawer to make it slide? Does it need a wipe over? Make it look as good as it can. A drawer that flows out will make you smile – it is a simple thing, but every little bit counts. If you are noticing your mind saying "FFS really? Do I have to?" YES YOU DO. Why? Because this is where the lowering of what you can have seeps in. Watch out for it. It will happen in all kinds of ways in your life. Where you know what you want, but you accept a lower version. This is not a Ferrari. It is a drawer. There are no reasons why you can't do it. Only that you are agreeing that is not worth the effort. If that happens here, it will happen everywhere.

Do you have a structure that helps you find what you need? There are some great organisers you can get to help with finding what you want with ease. Again, this may feel like overload, but I have my reasons. We are looking at how easy you can make your life doing the things that take time daily. If you spend 30 seconds finding a bra that you love, or a pair of knickers that you know are not in the washing bin… times that every day for a year and you are wasting...

Let's do the maths to really prove my point of how we can reduce wasted time and reclaim your life…

2 minutes daily to find something…

14 minutes a week – a workout/a cup of tea/ time to meditate…

12 hours and a bit over a year…

Looking for anything will make you open to an emotional response. It will agitate you and create more thinking around it. 'I am sure it is in here' 'I know it isn't in the washing' 'oh, did I wear it last week?'. All thinking is still thinking. Good or bad. Time is ticking and remember our goal is to get you doing what you love, as much as you can, EVERY DAY.

Cutting out spare moments is going to give you back time that you can spend where you want to, rather than agreeing that is it not available to you.

Step Two – Lay it all out.

Lay everything out on your bed to see clearly what you have. Look at it all and see all of those categories we looked at in section one. Go back and check to see what ones really resonated with you. There will be some that had a bigger influence than others. These are yours. We are often unaware of the heritage in stories. We are often influenced by our parents and grandparents about how we interpret our world. Our knickers and how we feel about them are impacted by how we were brought up and what we were told as children.

I tell you this to alleviate the responsibility that all you have in there is all about you and this lifetime. Nope. It can go back a long way. It can relate to how underwear was used as a weapon and a tool to both empower women and also disempower them. My goal is not to give you a history lesson, but to make you conscious that although this is your life, it may well have stories in it that have 'dinosaur shit' on them, they go back so far. And in so doing, they have no relevance to who you are today. But unless we look at all of those stories, they stay unconscious and as we discovered in Section One – we cannot change what we are not aware of.

What is in there that you just didn't know was there? Did you find surprises? Maybe found things you had been searching for? As we use our knicker drawer as our emotion space, there will be things in there that you felt were a safe place to put them. And the time in which they were put there may have expired their importance – are they still special?

Is there more in there than you thought?

How much of it do you not use?

These clarifying questions help in seeing how much excess energy you have that you are not using. If we decluttered the space and released the energy, just imagine what you could do with it. And if it is happening here, it will be happening in other areas of your life.

Use this space to write down what you are noticing and what you would use the extra energy/capacity to create in your life?

_____

_____

_____

_____

_____

_____

_____

Step three – Let your Mantra be your filter...

In the introduction I described how I wanted to feel. I decided that as I wanted a 'sexy, strong, lean' body, anything that didn't support that description in my head was out! It meant 75% of what was in there went.

So, the question is this again. How do *you* want to feel about your body?

I have a _____,_____ and _____ body!

This is your mantra. This is all about you. No one else's ideas are in here. Not mine or anyone else's business. This is about what you want to feel about who you are, and what you know to be true inside of you. This is the little girl in there saying I want to be_____! Not the grown-up girl who has an insta and Pinterest board, read too many magazines and watches so many 'look at me' type shows which tell her how to be and feel. This is noticing that and calling it on the bullshit it all is. This is YOUR life, and for this to be part of who you are and what you want to feel in this life with this body you have today, you need to appreciate all that it is.

Take a look in the mirror. What you have in front of you is who you are today, and *she is* the one we are talking about – not the figment of imagination that exists in books, films and old parts of history, that are not real in any way, shape, or form. They DO NOT exist. But we are so consumed by these figments, all day, every day, we cannot help but be impacted by them. The only way we can resist that is by putting in clear boundaries on where we spend our focus.

What do you allow into your mind? Being more conscious of what you allow in is going to be really helpful in making sure that when we clear things out, you are conscious enough not to let things back in. Algorithms in social media will always win, if you are unaware. Always. Mere mortals cannot fight against them. Please be conscious of what you let in, for how long and why. The why is THE most vital part here. Journal about what you do and why you do it. Often, I can find myself on a social media platform, from habit, or searching for a virtual hug. Ask more questions of your time and where you spend it and in section three, we will be looking at piecing back together what you now want to create with your new awareness.

Your *Mantra* is not what the outside world thinks you should wear or how your body feels.

Wear what feels right for you.

What suits your body type, and does it fit?

Does your underwear still feel great when you wear it for longer than five minutes?

Make a note of this. This is all about you. What each piece of underwear says is something reflective of you and what you want. Take notice of the reasons and decisions you have each for each item.

Your underwear is all about YOU. As you look at each piece, ask what you loved about it and make notes here. This list helps with what you want. It may be the colour – if you love black but think white makes a better statement, notice the narrative that is going on. Or if you want to wear red but feel this says 'slutty'… This list is all about what you LOVE in your drawer and finding out what you have and if we can take one titbit from each piece, we can make the puzzle of what you love clearer. This is the clarity piece we will need before we start to fill up the drawer again.

After speaking to an old friend recently about this book, she laughed as she reminded me of my horror that there were such things as period knickers! I had not been brought up with this notion at all and I didn't understand why you would not want to feel great in knickers at the time of the month when you feel your most vulnerable.

Or when I was dog walking and told an older friend who said she never understood why people even bothered with matching underwear and then stopped and said... 'oh, that says a lot about me, eh!' Yes, it does. It all does. In your underwear you will find many of the stories you have about how you run your life. This book is here to make these conscious for you, so you can then decide what *you* want. Often our thinking is enculturated patterns, driven from our ancestors. Working classes were not thinking about how beautiful their underwear was at all. It was all part of the functional wardrobe. We have evolved in many ways but there are pockets of stories that we keep passing down.

The Ends of the Ham and Thanksgiving

A husband asked his wife while preparing for their thanksgiving feast why she cut off the ends of the ham - a traditional meat for thanksgiving in the USA.

"I am not sure why, but my mum used to do it..." Bemused, the woman called her mother to probe into the story.

The woman telephones her mother.

"Hey muma, I need to ask you a question... are you having ham?"

"Yes we are, Nanna is here, and you know how she likes it."

"Oh great! I have a question about the ham. Pete asked me and I didn't know the answer... Muma, why do you cut the ends off the ham?"

The mother chuckled and paused. "Oh, I don't know. Nanna always did it, so I did. But she is here. Hold on" the mother

puts the phone aside, there is some nattering and chuckling in
the background and returns laughing.
"Well, you will not believe this... She said when her and
Grandpa were young, they were so poor they had a tiny oven
and tiny pans and no ham would ever fit. So, she had to cut off
the ends to fit it into the pan!"

It is a simple story, but it really helps to clarify that not all stories we take on board are horrible ones that make us squirm and want to change them. Some are just where we have taken on habits and rituals from others when were younger, less aware and not questioning. I want you to question E V E R Y T H I N G!

This book is about stopping and questioning why you do what you do. Does is work for you? Does it fit the life you lead today?

If not, look at how you can change it and if so, love it even more!

Write out some of what you are noticing about the knickers you currently have.

Colours I love:

Textures I adore:

Shapes that make me feel fabulous:

Types I love for occasions, including going out, staying in, period times…

Step Four – Let the zenning begin!

Now you have everything out. You have looked at what you want to keep and why. We need to release what is left. If you feel that this is going somewhere, it may feel easier to release. There are many charities now that take bras and knickers as they can go in the rag bags. Or you can use them as a filler for cushions.

Bags at the ready. This is the part where you may feel resistance. To be honest if you didn't, I would be more worried, as there are going to be stories attached. What I want you to do is to just *notice* them, like they are friends of yours, floating in with an opinion. Don't add any extra thinking to this. It is all about noticing it, rather than trying to fix how you feel about it. Just sit with the emotion. It *will* shift. No one has felt an emotion forever, right? So, breathe with it. Notice it. Stay curious and put the item where it needs to go.

Charity, Ebay, friends… where is its next home?

Section Review.

That's it for this section. It must now start to feel very different in your drawer. Clearing space is such an important part of the process and you have done that. The next section is about making sure we connect with what we refill it with and not just going back into old patterns - being sure of what we REALLY want in there and why it is important to us. We have journaled quite a bit in this session, but please just empty out any thoughts that are still rolling around. They are no use to you in there.

Journal below any thoughts that come up from what we have talked about.

Some words from a client of Kerry's

The title, 'Shift the Shit' (Kerry's programme, now called DeKluttered™), caught my attention because I've felt for a long time that I have lots of 'shit' crammed into both my head and my life, and I've wanted to deal with it and stop gathering so much!

So, I decided to take a leap of faith and see if this program could help. I block myself all the time from doing fun stuff, taking action that could help my business progress, help me to lose weight and so much more.

What I got from Kerry's program was wonderful. Part of her process is decluttering but it's not just tidying up. Taking what may seem like baby steps, but in reality, caused my world to shudder a little — in a really good way - I didn't just get to declutter.

I got to understand several of the deep and hidden reasons why I gather clutter in the first place and find it so difficult to get rid of it. Which is life changing. Because now I can never go back. Which is brilliant!

Through Kerry's wisdom and insight, I had a lightbulb moment in identifying a huge habit I have that contributes to me stopping myself, that I had never seen before. What I love is that bringing awareness to this now allows me to deal with it.

Thank you, Kerry, for your help and guidance. You're amazing xx

Anne-Marie

Section Three - What do you REALLY want?

In this third section we are building on what we have so far. Now we are going to get clear on how you decide what you want to put in. This is still a new change and so it may feel like I am being overly obvious about it all. This is done consciously on my part to really enforce the lesson that you **set the intentions in life,** and they come true. If you are not clear, something else will happen. You may get lucky and half like what the universe throws at you, but I know that when you are clear about what you want, the percentage of you getting it increases tenfold.

The gap between what you want and what you have is where you will find resentment and frustration. It will be masked in all kinds of overcompensating; over doing anything – anything - to dull the feelings you have about the lack in your life. Again, I want to re-emphasise kindness here. This is about noticing what you do with love because we take on so much unconsciously and become 'that' person. The role of this book is to encourage you to just look and see what you notice. Notice something that you do for maybe the first time and then realise you have regained a choice. So, you can choose to do something different. Be kind to yourself about it. Let go of what you think about why you did what you did. It is done. Gone. Now is the time to allow forgiveness and use the energy released to create what you want.

From section two you will have a drawer that is ready and feels beautiful. The only items now that are going in are those that adhere to your 'Mantra' and you adore all that is in there. If you are at all hesitant, now is the time for you to look again. If there are some that are not 100% yeses, put them aside for a while. When you feel what they are – stay or go - you can deal with them then. Remember, we are not having any compromise in there at all. Please go back and look again at what agreements you have about what is in there. The rules are: LOVE it! This is your drawer and what you do in here is such a reflective space for you and all that you do.

Are you are still finding it hard to love ALL of what it is in there? Or can't decide what you really want to have in there? Use this space to write out your considerations or just what you 'do' know. If there is friction, and you are compromising the rules, I need to remind you of something - your happiness depends on this. Yes, I know we are talking knickers, and that may sound dramatic. But if you cannot be ruthless with what you wear on your bits, what hope do we have for anything more in life?

Write out below anything that is getting in the way of you loving what you have left in the drawer.

Once you have written out what your considerations are, it will help to see what the gap is. The gap between where you are now, what you have written and where you want to be.

Compromise gets you a lot of what you want... PLUS a lot of what you do not. It is not intentional. It is going for the easy way out but disappoints the little girl in you. She doesn't want to do that. At all. You are not convincing anyone. The energy will shine through no matter how much you say 'it's ok'. It is NOT.

What do you want to put in there?

This is a big decision and is really connected to who are you today. How do you feel about your body and what it is doing for you now and what it has already done for you? Coming from a place of appreciation will connect you with loving your body and deepening the connection you have to who you are and what you want to create in life.

What do you want to create in with this life you have?

_____

_____

_____

_____

_____

_____

_____

What have you learnt so far? Who are you trying to please in what you wear?

_____

_____

_____

_____

_____

_____

Let's revisit your mantra for a bit. My Mantra is to feel sexy, lean and strong. When I buy underwear, this is the mantra that goes along with it. Does it mean that I do not have white seamless knickers in there? No, they are great for jeans. Do I keep them when they go grey? Nope. They go. The lesson to be ruthless with what you want is vital here. The point is that I want you to look at what you really need for the life you lead – with the idea of it being the best it can be. A five pack of average knickers may be ok – but is it really what you aspire to?

What do you want? Pause here for a minute.

Ask…

What do you seek? Who am I, under 'it' all? What do I REALLY want?

And breathe.

Leave space for your intuition to check in. Feel it in your body. Feel there is something larger than us. I do not believe in a doctrine, but I do believe in values of kindness and love and we are all connected – Karma is a way I love to feel about the morals and values I have. I treat the world with as much kindness as I can – I share the love I have for being here, at this time, with as many people as I can. And when I am not feeling kind, I have tools, mostly to stop sharing my shit, but that is book number two…

Section Review.

This section is about deepening the connection to who you are without the old stuff cluttering your head. Asking the questions that may feel simple in their delivery, but asking them of yourself. Noticing and seeing who you are, here, today, now. Are you creating a life that surrounds you with love and connection to this body and mind?

If there is a disconnect through your mind and body it will show up. Not in a nice neat little package, but in a compromise. A pleasing. A following of others. The result will be a little smidgen of resentment that can last a lifetime. This book is a chance to pause that. To reflect. To renew. And to release old, unfaithful patterns that no longer serve you and who you are today.

Below, please sit and allow yourself to write out any new thoughts that this section has brought forward. Things that you may never have thought you would be noticing in a book about knickers. But you knew, deep down, that there was always going to be more to your drawer, and I want you to allow that to come out here. Release it all. Why not? What would you have to lose by just letting it all out? All the considerations you have, even about this little book that asks too many questions. Because we both know it is not about the book...

The next section is about how our choices reflect our values and by knowing this, we can consciously create a life that soothes us. See you there.

Some words from a client of Kerry's

I consider myself to be an organised type of person, but life had thrown me some curve balls in recent years and I'd drifted into organised chaos!

I could lay my hands on anything I needed, but I was running to stand still with trying to keep on top of everything and prioritise what really needed to be done.

Kerry really is like some sort of fairy godmother who waves her wand and tells you firmly that you shall go to the ball!

Genuinely, she helped me to feel like I CAN do the things I need to do, when, where, with whom and how I need to do them!

Heather

Living a full and honest life takes courage, a willingness to have uncomfortable conversations and take action, and a bucket full of humour. Kerry brings all of these qualities to the table/walk & talk sessions. She is wise, she is bold and she has years of experience supporting people as they move and shift through all manner of life changing experiences.

Kerry was one of my go to supporters when my world completely changed a few years ago. To this day, she is someone I trust and turn to when I'm looking to break through my next layer of resistance.

Katy H

Section Four - Where's the fun in that?

_____

This section is your values and how your choices reflect them. Or how they do not. It is very simple. From the last section, you can see these more clearly when you look at each piece of clothing you have in your life. From this we can learn so much about you and what you want in your life:

How 'safe' a life you have created.

The risks you take, or don't.

The old stories you still love that keep you from living today.

The possible stories you want to be real.

The way in which you live in such a small amount of your life – i.e., how many pairs do you really wear?

The past ones that you keep in hope… of fitting into that old life, being her… the one who is still in there but not allowed out very often…

This is all about unleashing the devil-may-care attitude. We all have her in there, where you know you can be her and don't care if anyone else likes it or not. You love it and it makes you feel all you want to feel about yourself – that is the most important thing. They are your knickers and yet you still hold back. We still hold onto the acculturated patterns in us. The ones where we are the girl who has matching knickers because the image that the media portrays is that SHE has so much fun. She lives the life you want to lead.

Not anymore. Call out all the 'what if {insert name of the one you have in your head who is the most 'judgey' of all} sees and thinks {insert what is your biggest fear}'. We all have this, and this is never going to get you a life you want. It is **your** underwear. Yours. As is your life. It is only there for you to see and whomever you choose to see it. It is your safe space and yet we still conform. We still play the part of the external wants.

What do you want to wear? Who do you want to see in the mirror? If your Mantra is not in alignment with her in the mirror – something has to change. Be it your reality of who you are now, in this time, age and body, or the who you want to see in the mirror. Who do you want to be? What is the gap?

What would be fun? Why can't your first part of getting dressed be one that makes you smile? Why not be that for everything? But let's start with your underwear - we can build from there. Rules are there for you to live by – what do you want? No one else gives a flying fart! Honestly, they do not. No one. If you are arguing the case, this will have come at a cost to you. Love you and let go of what you 'think' others 'think'. You are more than likely to be wrong.

Follow me for a minute about this. Do you think that anyone knows what you are currently thinking? And if we follow that – do you 'think' that you can 'out-think' what you 'think' others are thinking – so you can act according to what you 'think' they 'think'? And then discover they don't! It is such a huge waste of your time on this planet. Yes, it is wasteful to invest your limited time on the planet on shit that you cannot change. No one in the world has ever changed someone else's thinking by trying to outthink what they should or should not do.

And if you are acting from overthinking… or you 'think' you are. I will also go as far as saying 'bbbbbuuulllshhiitt'. Yes, there, I said it. It is not about that either. Yes I know I just said that in the last paragraph and yes it is true. But the crazy thing it is not about them at all. It is what you know to be true about *you* and you may be scared to be you. To really put you out there in the world as you. So using others 'imagined thoughts' as truth gives you permission to not do what you want. To stay 'safe' and hiding.

But. Sorry I need to take you a little further down the rabbit hole for a moment. Hiding from what? From whom? You? Or your thoughts about what you think others think of you and what that means to you? This is the nub of it all. You are here. This is your time. And if you are unconscious of doing something because you are unaware of the impact, for sure you will carry on. But this is a 'STOP THAT SHIT AND

LISTEN' moment. This is your time. You are here. You were put here for some weird old reason, and it is your own responsibility to live it. And to put in support mechanisms to make sure you keep on that track of doing just that. To enjoy your weirdly wonderful human self. To let go of the attachment to your thinking and to act and be you.

Living in the hope of thinking what you wear reflects what others think about you will not lead to inner joy. It will lead you to running a life that does not support you – the little girl inside. She will just be wearing her mother's knickers and wondering what the fuck happened to her.

To give you some more clarity in understanding you, let's take a few minutes and play with values. I find this a fascinating way to learn more about what drives me, and I hope it does the same for you.

Journal Exercise:

What are your values?

I really want you to complete this. Don't just read it and think hmmm, yeah that is me. It is a process and to get the most out of it you are going to have to do it.

Here is a list – not exclusive at all. I want you to circle your **top ten**, or even just start with ones that mean a lot to you, then reduce to ten, then double ring around the top five and then triple ring the top three.

- Freedom
- Security
- Loyalty
- Intelligence
- Connection
- Creativity
- Humanity
- Success
- Respect
- Invention
- Diversity
- Generosity
- Integrity
- Finesse
- Love
- Openness
- Religion
- Order
- Advancement
- Respect
- Joy/Play
- Forgiveness
- Work Smarter not Harder
- Excitement
- Entrepreneurial

- Change
- Goodness
- Involvement
- Faith
- Wisdom
- Beauty
- Caring
- Peace
- This Too Shall Pass Attitude
- Honesty
- Adventure
- Kindness
- Teamwork
- Career
- Communication
- Learning
- Excellence
- Innovation
- Quality
- Commonality
- Contributing
- Spiritualism
- Strength
- Entertain
- Happiness

- Wealth
- Speed
- Power
- Affection
- Cooperation
- Love of Career
- Friendship/Relationship
- Encouragement
- Family
- Clarity
- Fun-Loving
- Charisma
- Humour
- Leadership
- Renewal
- Home
- Be True
- Contentment
- Friendship
- Courage
- Balance
- Compassion
- Fitness
- Professionalism
- Harmony

- Relationship
- Knowledge
- Patience
- Change
- Prosperity
- Wellness
- Finances
- Gratitude
- Grace
- Endurance
- Facilitation
- Effectiveness
- Fun
- Fame
- Justice
- Appreciation
- Willingness
- Trusting Your Gut
- Giving People a Chance
- Patience
- Forgiveness
- Self-Respect
- Abundance
- Reciprocity
- Enjoyment

My top three values are:

1. _____

2. _____

3. _____

Top value number **one** is: Describe what this value means to you in your own words and how it shows up in your life currently.

_____

_____

_____

_____

_____

_____

_____

Now say, if you were more connected to it, how else would it show up?

_____

_____

_____

_____

_____

_____

Top value number **two** is: Describe what this value means to you in your own words and how it shows up in your life currently.

_____

_____

_____

_____

_____

_____

Now say, if you were more connected to it, how else would it show up?

_____

_____

_____

_____

_____

_____

_____

Top value number **three** is: Describe what this value means to you in your own words and how it shows up in your life currently.

_____

_____

_____

_____

_____

_____

_____

Now say, if you were more connected to it, how else would it show up?

_____

_____

_____

_____

_____

_____

Would it be obvious to those who know you?

Now tell me where you think those same values are compromised. I know it is uncomfortable but let's be honest with each other. This book is about you. If you are not willing to write it down, then it will stay the same. Let go of what has happened and what hasn't happened because of you not standing up for your values.

_____

_____

_____

_____

_____

_____

_____

_____

_____

_____

_____

_____

_____

"Values are like fingerprints, nobody's are the same,
but you leave them all over everything you do."
Elvis Presley

Section Review.

This section is about understanding and valuing the importance of reviewing your values frequently. Especially when you have had a significant life change. For example, in a serious relationship, creating a family, a move away, overcoming a death in the family, a job or career change, a decade birthday... Any life shock can make you change your life instantly.

As soon as my first son was born, I described the feeling as 'same world, different planet'. Everything changed in a moment, and my values with it. Family became a much higher value for me, even though this had not played a huge part in my upbringing as I come from a family with a lot of grief and loss. This became the forerunner of what my life was about. It will, of course, change and develop over time. The rule is to keep conscious of changes in your life that have an impact on life 'style'.

The importance of understanding this is vital to find what the gaps are in your life. Know your values, how they appear and what happens if you compromise them.

Our next section is pulling it all together to a life you LOVE - not just like or tolerate. Using intention as your tool for transformation, you can create a life you love in all areas.

Get ready.

Some words from a client of Kerry's

 Before starting Kerry's programme, I was feeling stuck in my life and thought patterns. I was hopeful that it would help but had my reservations as I had tried a lot of things over the previous 15 years or so without much success, from counselling, to numerous self-help books, to hypnotherapy.

After the first session, I made a list of areas I wanted to focus on and looking back at them now, I am amazed to see that I have addressed or made steps towards addressing all of them already.

I have certainly felt different since starting the programme and now I realise why... the changes have been incremental so I haven't been consciously aware of all of them. They are part of my 'new normal'.

I'm discovering new things about myself as well as rediscovering some long forgotten things, and I don't feel the same despondency and distress as I did before starting the programme. Instead, I am feeling a sense of inner peace and I'm becoming more focused on creating the life and future that I want.

I now realise that I am my own expert, but the insight and support from both Kerry and other group members is proving invaluable. Things are sinking in in a way that they haven't before and I'm so, so grateful, both that I found the course, and to Kerry, for putting it together.

Thank you, Sharon

5

Section Five - Do you love it all?

In this section, we are talking about intention; what it is, what it isn't and how to use it to create a life you love.

Most of our lives we live in the *hope* that things will change, and yes, there is a natural cause and effect in life that will invoke change. When creating a conscious change we are setting our **intention.** Setting your intention is being clear on what you want to create through your actions. It is being connected to the outcome and being clear on what that means for you and the 'why' it brings with it.

The 'why' you do something is vital and, as you discovered in section four in reaffirming your values, the why comes from what in that is for you in real terms - how do those values play out in real life for you.

Being clear on what you want, and asking for it, will take courage and the confidence to say it. In this section we are breaking down what that means for you and how, by connecting some proverbial dots, it will be easier for you to:

firstly, know how vitally important this for you; and

secondly, what to look for when you are not following what you love.

What do you love?

Not such a funny question to think about your underwear but now we need to expand on this further into other areas of your life.

Keep it simple

I want you to look at four areas of your life and then to get clear on:

what you have that isn't working in them;

what you want in them;

what makes it really clear to you, through your values, that it shows how much you love your life.

Do this for each of the following four areas. All four combined will help you simplify where you need to focus some attention and bring in more of what you love and noticing what you don't and letting that go.

I am excited for you to now further the transformation. The first area I want you look at is:

Surroundings

Just like the drawer, I want you to look at what you have in it.

Start by just feeling what the word 'surroundings' mean to you? What you are surrounded by can be changed with a little focus and a bit of effort. Start close by. What are you surrounded by physically where you are now? Then, gradually move your focus further and further out. Out to where you live: your town, your county, your country. Take in what it means to you and how it supports who you are or who you are not.

How do you currently feel about your surroundings? Noticing the impact. Are you making it 'ok', even though it does not to feel right? This is all part of the agreement that you can't have what you want.

But you can. Firstly, we need to get clear on what is and isn't working. Use the prompts below to get a clearer picture on what you already have that is working and what isn't.

Write below what you love currently about your surroundings:

Home

Work

Bedroom

Town

_____

Country

_____

Write out what you know you are compromising and where are you not in line with your values?

_____

The second area I want you to look at is:

Money

In the Knicker Drawer, money is the way in which we invest in ourselves. The agreed currency we use as humans is money. And energy has an impact on that. One of my favourite books is Denise Duffield Thomas's *Get Rich Lucky Bitch,* and she is very much aligned to my feelings about how you create a life you love.

When you are creating, it is vital to look at how you *feel* about money and the stories you have connected to it. Is there a flow? Think of how we made a place for everything in your drawer and how, once we cleared it out, we knew what everything was there for and that it was loved and used.

The same can be said for money. But the stories attached to money run deep. Here we are just going to look at what is and isn't working. Sometimes we need to notice that what bad habits we have to change them.

For example, if you look at your normal expenditure on 'coffee on the go', and you have one on the way to work and one at lunch, this habit can be costly and the initial feeling of it being a treat is way past its sell by date. Now it is just a habit. And that 'old habit' could fund a new habit that is much more aligned to how you want your life to feel today; A yoga class, or investing in a book or a course to change the way you think and feel.

Write out below where you know your money habits are NOT supporting your life?

_____

_____

_____

_____

_____

_____

_____

Home

_____

_____

_____

_____

_____

Work

_____

_____

_____

_____

_____

Bedroom

Write out what you know you are currently compromising and are not in line with your values?

The third area to explore is your:

Relationships

In the Knicker Drawer, we discovered that the most important relationship is the one we have with ourself. Now, by broadening this agreement, what else is there for you to look at in your relationships?

Start close by and work your way out further. It may help to write a list of all those who may not be 'in' your current life, but still have an impact on it.

Home

Work

Bedroom

Write out what you know you are currently compromising and are not in line with your values?

The final area we are going to cover:

Health and Emotions

In the Drawer, it was about the feelings we had that meant we were keeping hold of a past or a future that no longer served us. For this section, we are going to use what you have learnt and put it to use.

Any area above that you are merely tolerating or isn't aligned to you will include a compromise on your part. This book is to make you aware of these and then to ask you to clarify what you REALLY do want, instead putting up with what you currently have. In the Drawer, to just look at what was there initially before we started to work on it was an essential part of this.

Home

Work

Bedroom

Write out what you know you are currently compromising and are not in line with your values?

Section Review.

In this section we are finally coming out of the knicker drawer and looking at how what we have learnt in there can now be applied elsewhere in our lives, and to feel the impact it can have to transform so much more.

It is my intention this section started to highlight other areas where you may have compromised in the past. And now, with this new awareness, you can see why you felt like you did about situations. Now you know the cost it has, you can decide what you want to change. Don't make a huge list, it will feel overwhelming and that in itself will stop you. We just want slow and steady.

Think tortoise not hare.

Some words from a client of Kerry's

 If you are looking for someone to be in your corner no matter what, Kerry is the coach for you.

I say corner, but actually I should say in your cosmos because her reach is deep. If you have committed to change, Kerry will match you, positive charge for positive charge. Bring yourself and she will feed you the good stuff she has learned on her own path.

18 months ago, I was 4 stone overweight, facing redundancy from a job I was bored of and struggling with low mood. The moods still come and go but the fat is gone and I'm on a path I believe in again.

Kerry has been in my cosmos throughout.

Bring her into yours.

Sarah P

6

Section Six - What do you REALLY want from now on...

Here we are. At the end of the book and pulling it all together. I am thrilled you got this far. It means you now have the means to free up energy in your life, to transform it how you choose.

You also now know what your top values are and why these are so important to you. So, when you are feeling just out of sorts, start with looking over your values. It will give you a filter to look though. And where they are out of alignment, it will assist you in getting back into flow, movement or just wanting to do whatever it is you 'think' you want to do.

Procrastination is never about you not wanting to do what you say you want. It is about not wanting to do the thing it will take to get that shit done. How can you use this book to overcome this? Simply put in place the things we have asked for you to do in your knicker drawer.

Let's recap.

Lesson One:

Stop and take a good look around. Take it all in and see what you notice. Ask what is and isn't working so you can start off the process of change from being incompetent to competent.

Lesson Two:

Declutter. This is the part where, after you have noticed what is and isn't working, you go in and clear it out So you are then left with what is still working for you – what you can use today that helps you love your life and create a life you continue to love.

Lesson Three:

What do you want? Deepening the connection to who you are today will allow you to create a deeper appreciation for you, what you have, and to feel gratitude. The lesson is really about asking for what you want in a way, so as you get it.

Lesson Four:

When our values are compromised there is a cost. It may be that it is the cost of what it takes to make us feel ok about it, but there is a cost. And it may appear in all kinds of areas. Look for the overcompensating, the numbing, the avoidance. Think of it as a stream, flowing freely. If there are obstacles, there will be pockets of stagnant water, a branch will then attract more twigs, which will attract reeds and more and more water will be stopped in its flow. Fish will get caught. Our lives are very similar. I know we are supposed to be the most evolved but, in some areas, our intellect gets in the way. Our thinking can be detrimental to our happiness.

Lesson Five:

We can now use the knowledge we have to be able to create a life you love in all areas. This is now more than your knicker drawer. It is about who you want to be in all areas of your life and how, by looking at your knicker drawer and sorting through it, using our steps you can move this into other areas of your life that will have a bigger impact too.

And there you have it. One refreshed and revitalised life, ready to go with more energy available for you to use.

I wish you so much joy from this book. You really can decide to choose to have fun. No matter how hard life can be, it can also be fun. You can find a place to enjoy the learning. The knickers part of this book was to make you chuckle and laugh as you learn and my intention was to get you to start to think differently about your life and see that there are many ways you can live it. There is only one you and there is only one chance.

I hope for now you start to do that more.

And one last thing. I would love, if you have enjoyed this book, please share it.

Some words from a client of Kerry's

During my lockdown experience I happened upon a declutter workshop run by Kerry.

In all honesty, I only joined it because I needed the distraction (I usually work non-stop and I couldn't) and I needed to declutter- perfect! I ran around and completed the course taking before and after photos wow you should have seen the difference.

Little did I know that the amazing Kerry would start to encourage other differences in so many other areas of my life than just dealing with the stuff in it!

I had enjoyed myself so much that I signed on to SHIFT THE SHIT (now DeKluttered™), obviously a natural progression. I had bonded with the wonderful women in the group; we had a safe space to share and go on the next journey together.

This gave me time to start implementing the things that I had thought I would get around to one day. It meant I started to stop and think about me - how often do we truly do that? I am at the tip of the ice berg with how much more I want to develop and I know that Kerry has my hand, heart and head and will guide me through safely to a beautiful me. Who wouldn't want that?

There are other coaches out there but when you find the mentor who is willing to talk straight so that you can actually get shit done and start enjoying a better life, hold onto her because it's going to be an awesome journey. And

77

you will never be able to thank her enough for gaining your freedom, your soul, the life you are meant to live back!!

Thank you, Kerry. I truly look forward to working with you again.

Sam

How I can help

The best way for you to learn more about how we can work together, is to visit my website. You will also find how to connect with me on my social media channels and find all my free stuff! www.Kerryhales.com

A little extra for you.

If you go to www.lifelessonsfromyourknickerdrawer.com I have created something just for you to do after reading this book, to embed and take forward what you have learnt. It is a 90 day declutter your life plan, with a personal video from me to talk you through it and also 10 days of journal prompts to help you continue to live a DeKluttered™ life. And of course, it is fun.

linkedin.com/in/kerryhales
facebook.com/kerryhalescoach
instagram.com/kerry_hales